Lying with the Heavenly Woman

ALSO BY ROBERT A. JOHNSON

He: Understanding Masculine Psychology

She: Understanding Feminine Psychology

We: Understanding the Psychology of Romantic Love

Inner Work: Using Dreams and Active Imagination for Personal Growth

Ecstasy: Understanding the Psychology of Joy

Femininity Lost and Regained

Transformation: Understanding the Three Levels of Masculine Consciousness

Owning Your Own Shadow: Understanding the Dark Side of the Psyche

The Fisher King and the Handless Maiden: Understanding the Wounded Feeling Function in Masculine and Feminine Psychology

Lying with the Heavenly Woman

Understanding and Integrating the Feminine Archetypes in Men's Lives

ROBERT A. JOHNSON

HarperSanFrancisco
A Division of HarperCollins*Publishers*

Book design by Lisa Dordal

FIRST EDITION

Library of Congress Cataloging-in-Publication Data

Johnson, Robert A., 1921–

Lying with the heavenly woman : understanding and integrating the feminine archetypes in men's lives / Robert A. Johnson.

p. cm.

ISBN 0-06-251065-7.—ISBN 0-06-251066-5 (pbk)

1. Men—Psychology. 2. Femininity (Psychology) 3. Archetype (Psychology) 4. Anima (Psychoanalysis) 5. Masculinity (Psychology) I. Title.

BF692.5.J64 1994

155.3'32—dc20 93-39206

CIP

ISBN 0–06–251065–7 (cloth)

ISBN 0–06–251066–5 (pbk)

ISBN 0–06–251102–5 (int'l pbk)

94 95 96 97 98 ❖ RRD(H) 10 9 8 7 6 5 4 3 2 1

This edition is printed on acid-free paper that meets the American National Standards Institute Z39.48 Standard.

Contents

Lying with the Heavenly Woman

INTRODUCTION:

Femininity in a Man's Life

The relationship of man to woman and to his own femininity has been regulated throughout most of history by law, custom, convention. Only recently has man gained the capacity for personal decisions in these matters, a very great step in evolution. This freedom is as new as our modern world and brings some demands on consciousness that have never been experienced before.

The paths that were stable and reliable for primitive man and in most of the world even today are now for modern man paths of uncertainty and offer so many choices that we are bewildered. In earlier times a man married under his parents' direction, lived a household life that was almost completely stereotyped, and rarely, if ever, inquired into the concept of freedom in these matters. You may as well ask a man in any of the traditional societies to exercise freedom in his relationship to gravity as to expect freedom in his marriage. I have never known a traditional Hindu to question whether his marriage was fulfilling to him or even if he was happy in it. Such questions rarely arise in traditional societies. Evolution waited for our own times to introduce freedom into relationship. Since he has grasped the white-hot stuff of freedom, modern man must have an equally powerful grasp of consciousness if he is to avoid the pitfalls that are so common in our relationships today.

A man facing the heady prospect of freedom in the realm of relationship to feminine elements in the world—both inside and outside himself—must have some specific information and gain an extraordinary degree of differentiation if he is to avoid the pitfalls that characterize our time. As we shall see in an African tale of the double anima, the heavenly woman figures as a heavenly vision that can overpower a young man, who becomes like Tristan entering the Grail Castle too soon. In this story an informed and clear differentiation between the light anima and the earthy, human anima makes all the difference. It is this quest for absolute clarity in meeting these vital feminine elements that is our subject.

Few men understand how important femininity is in their lives, both inner and outer. Almost all of a man's sense of value, worth, safety, joy, contentment, belongingness, and happiness derive from his inner feminine nature. If God created male and female and gave them equal power (I like to translate the critical word *rib* as "side" or "half" in the Genesis story of the creation of Eve), the delicate and subtle half that is the province of femininity is as powerful as the masculine province. Men, in their arrogance, generally think it is their strength, possessions, and dominations that bring them happiness. But it is not so. Happiness is feminine in a man, a feeling quality, and generally mysterious to him.

Without good masculinity, a man is weak, ineffective, and useless; but it is femininity that inspires his strength, meaning, and value. He is likely to look both inward and outward for this elusive quality, and we will find both inner and outer femininity in our search. Inner aspects of femininity in a man are difficult for him to comprehend since we live in a culture not well equipped to examine such things; the outer aspects—his mother, wife, sister, daughter—are easier to identify.

Our Western patriarchal culture has been built on a model that has produced one of the most advanced civilizations ever to exist. Our science, high material standard of living, greatly expanded capacities of travel and communication, the great vista of the twentieth century—all these have been won at the cost of disregard for another faculty, that of feeling. There is little room for the feeling function in a society that worships rationality and abstraction as deeply as we do. Coolness and objectivity are absolutely required for the scientific pursuit. The term *abstract* comes from the Greek *ab,* "to move away from," and *strahere,* "to stand." We must stand at least a little apart from any subject to make an abstract relationship to it. And that standing apart instantly wounds the feeling function. Put more simply, one cannot accomplish disciplined tasks if one listens to the feeling function. The cool world of abstraction has no place for the warm world of feeling. Every woman suffers this lack of feeling from her man—both inner and outer—and is mostly inarticulate in her complaint of the one-sidedness of modern life. Men become feeling-barren when they school themselves in the modern arts of abstraction and rationality.

Sanskrit, that feeling-rich language that is the basis of most East Indian tongues, has ninety-six terms for love. Ancient Persian has eighty. Greek has three. And we have only one. The Eskimo language has thirty words for snow since snow is such a vital element in their lives. If we had thirty words for relationship, we would be better equipped to observe that important dimension of our lives.

Certainly this is prime evidence that feeling and relationship are the inferior functions in our society. Lack of language for any subject means lack of interest in that area. We build wonderful Boeing 747s and atomic generators, but we build very poor marriages and relationships. We stand in severe danger that our Brave New World of mechanical marvels may be overturned by the poor quality of the feeling function that has accompanied it.

One can tell at a glance from the feminine figures in a man's dreams what relationship he has to happiness and a sense of well-being in his life. If the women in his dreams are happy and relate well to him, he will be happy. If they are ill or weak or angry, he will have little or no sense of well-being. I know of no other single element that has so much to do with a man's happiness.

Dr. Jung once analyzed for his students a series of dreams of a very gifted man. One dream was that a woman came into the room, put her hands to her head, moaned, and left. "Now he will catch it!" observed Dr. Jung. If a man's inner woman disapproves and walks out on him, things will go badly in his feeling life and his sense of worth. In the Mahabharata, the great Hindu epic poem, there is a terrible moment when the king has slighted the Shakti (an embodiment of the feminine principle of the universe); her reply is to close the seven portals of her body, compress her breath, and shoot out of the top of her head, returning to the formless universe from which she came. All the male elements of the whole kingdom are bereft at the loss of the feminine principle and are in a state of mourning. Sad is the man whose Shakti has left him because he has offended her.

It also follows that good contact with the interior woman will make it much easier to be on good terms with the exterior women of one's life. Finally we must admit that we are talking about femininity in its profound aspect, which cannot be divided into interior and exterior aspects. But until we earn the right to this unity, we had best make careful differentiation of the inner and outer. Goethe, in his masterpiece *Faust,* ends the great drama with the words "The Eternal Femininc leads us on." This is the view of a mature man who had earned the right to a unified view of femininity. This maturity cost Goethe a lifetime of highly conscious inner work. *Faust* is the best guide we have in Western literature for this work. This account of a great soul journey can best be read as Goethe's autobiography; in it he outlines the steps he followed to come to terms with the actual women in his story and with his interior feminine nature. This is modern man laid out in contemporary language for our guidance. We may be grateful for Goethe's instruction in this art.

It is immediately obvious that femininity is the color and delight and animation of a man's life. Without femininity a man is poverty-stricken and without life. *She* is life. Though there are many, many forms of relating to that life-giving principle, they all have their basis in femininity.

A Persian myth tells this story in a touching manner: In the beginning God made a beam of light that went streaking through space in its free, unencumbered way. It was perfect mobility and delight. God also made a clod of earth and set it, immobile, in space, where it was in perfect joy at its changeless feminine way. This went on for many eons before the inevitable happened. The beam of light ran into the clod of earth and became embedded in it. The beam of light cried out in dismay at its imprisonment and the clod of earth gasped in terror at the quickening that had occurred in its serene life. But both were irrevocably committed to this new life. The offspring of this union was the melon, which embodied both the material element of life and the ethereal beam of light that transfused it. All of creation, say the Persians, came from this melon.

This story is telling us that without the feminine, a man is an impotent beam of light streaking his ethereal way through the heavens but without any creativity.

Many words are revered in our language—such as *salvation* and *redemption*—and I wish to add a new one that is equally necessary for modern man. That is *differentiation,* the art of clarity, of unmuddling. If one had the various contents of the kitchen—salt, pepper, sugar, vinegar, spices, and so on—all mixed together in one indiscriminate mess, he could not proceed with any cooking. If a workman had all his tools dumped into one sack with the sharp ones and the dull ones and the wet ones and the dry ones indiscriminately mixed, he could not work properly. Psychologically speaking, lack of differentiation and clarity brings similar problems in a man's feminine life. I don't know of any element that cries for differentiation more than our attitudes toward femininity. If a man managed his office as indiscriminately as he generally manages his interior life, he would be bankrupt in a month. It is not surprising that our culture is largely bankrupt in relatedness for this very reason.

The feminine world is notoriously difficult to differentiate, for it is diffuse by nature and resists form and order. It is the duty of femininity to blur the edges of masculine form and bring softness and relativity. This is warmth and delight—but only if contained and kept safe within sufficient masculine form and order.

If a man muddles his mother complex with his wife, the household will be in chaos. If he muddles his concept of anima and daughter, he will wound the daughter very deeply. If he cannot tell the difference between wife and daughter, another tragedy is in the making. Each of these aspects of femininity is a healthy and holy quality in its own right; but mixed, they make a lethal brew. Many men have only one vague muddled attitude toward femininity. Nothing but trouble can issue from such an unholy mix.

In olden days these elements were nicely sorted out for us by tradition and law. There was a right way to do everything in life. Usually a man depended on his wife to make decisions in the feminine department; she deferred to him in masculine things. There is much to be said for this manner of living, but evolution has taken us past this simple solution. Man demands freedom in his inner world, and, especially these days, women demand their own masculine self-determination. The old days of authority are gone. There was little freedom but much safety; authority informed our lives and made most decisions for us. We have abandoned authority as the center of our lives, so we must rely on differentiation and clarity to make intelligent decisions in our modern world.

PART ONE:

The Feminine Elements

Let us look at the principal feminine elements—inner and outer—that make up a man's feminine nature. A careful examination will bring still more feminine elements to light, but here we consider only the principal ones. Then we can speak of the unholy mixtures that often follow when a man does not keep them clear and differentiated. Most of the suffering in a man's life stems from these unholy mixtures. They are lethal.

The principal forms of femininity that a man experiences in his life are the mother, the mother complex, the mother archetype, the sister, the anima, the wife, the daughter, sophia, the hetaira, friendship, and femininity in its homoerotic form—indeed, all the noble elements of feeling, wisdom, and relatedness in a man's life. We will examine each of these aspects of femininity in turn.

The Mother

Every man has a human being who is his mother—a finite personal being with all her characteristics, idiosyncrasies, virtues, and faults. She is probably the most powerful person in his whole life since she gave him his physical structure, fed and raised him, and largely determined his idea of women for the rest of his life. He is utterly dependent upon her in his early years, when she is life itself to him. Later he separates from her, but she always remains "Mom." Godmothers or substitute mothers or even institutions as mother may play a large part in his life, but they are only extensions of that human woman who is his mother. The chief characteristic to be observed is that she is personal and human. In our examination of femininity we must be reminded many times that the mother is "out there," a discrete human being.

The Mother Complex

Without any question, the mother complex is the most difficult encounter any man ever faces. It is the regressive capacity in him and will destroy his life more quickly than any other single element in his psychology. For a male to succumb to the mother complex is to lose the battle of life. The mother complex is his wish to regress to infancy again and to be taken care of, to crawl into bed and pull the covers over his head, to evade some responsibility that faces him. It can come as a mood, as a discouragement, as a paralysis, or as just being "fed up" with it all.

In Western mythology, the mother complex is represented by the dragon that every hero has to face and conquer. Mythology, old and new, has terrible stories of the hero being attacked by a fire-breathing dragon and his narrow victory over the monster. The fair maiden awaits him only after the dragon or mother complex has been conquered. Our Western myth of the Grail and the stories around King Arthur are excellent descriptions of the adolescent elements of dragon fighting.[1]

The first task in approaching the mother complex is to understand that it is not one's actual mother. Almost no youth is clear about what he is fighting when this part of his life demands attention, and he is likely to take it out on Mom, the actual woman who is his mother. Just to know

1. See my book *He: Understanding Masculine Psychology,* revised edition (New York: Harper & Row, 1989), the chronicle of a young man freeing himself of his mother complex.

that it is not anyone "out there" who is making the trouble is to be prepared for the real battle, always inward. Mom is a discrete human being "out there," while a man's mother complex is always an interior matter. This battle is precipitated by a man's tendency to give up or take refuge in the thousand excuses that any man can produce; this is the great danger of the mother complex.

A youth has done the hardest part of his dragon battle when he is consciously able to say, most of me wants that college degree, a small part of me thinks it is complete nonsense, a medium-sized part of me just wants to run away and not face the issue, and a small part of me wants to do whatever I am told is right. A youth is in good relationship to life if his mother complex (the part of him that wants to run away and not face the issues) occupies a minority of his energy. If it occupies a higher percentage, then he will need to do much inner work to bring his energies into some constructive focus. In any case, it is honesty and clarity that will allow the youth to bring his best energies under his conscious direction and not have warfare in his interior life.

I remember an incident in my own life that galvanized this kind of honesty and forced me to ask myself some questions that immediately brought clarity to my direction in life. I had followed the advice of aptitude tests and parents and enrolled in engineering school. One day a professor looked at one of my engineering drawings and with one simple question broke through the haze of confusion in my mind concerning vocation. He asked, "Do you like engineering?" My mother complex could not stand such a finely differentiated question and my budding career as an engineer vanished in this atmosphere of directness. I remember so vividly sitting down on a concrete step outside the professor's office. The dragon battle that immediately followed that question was the collision between docile obedience to authority in my life and my own sense of vocation. Answering that simple question with a direct *no* instantly led to the next clarification of my life. When I could see clearly what was mother complex in me—a passive acceptance of authority in order to gain safety—and what was my own individual character, then I could make a clear differentiation of who I was and what my true vocation might be. A far more mature man got up from that concrete step half an hour later.

This story sounds like an account of a collision between an inner part of my nature and the outer world. But the dragon battle is always between progressive and regressive forces within one's self. Dr. Jung used to pound on the table and say, "It is always a matter of *who,* never a matter of *what.*"

When I understood who I was in my dragon battle, then it was relatively easy to face the practicalities of what to do.

The bravado and bantam-rooster behavior of any young male is a product of his fright at the impending dragon battle that faces him. If he thinks the battle is "out there," he will make the most ridiculously blustering attempts at settling it "out there." He has to have "in here" settled before he can make the slightest progress "out there." Most young men saddle their psychological horses, make a brave foray "out there," fail (because they did not have the dragon settled inside), and then have to face that awful moment inside when the balance scale of life or death tips back and forth. It is the mother complex that is the death-dealing element in life. This is the true dragon battle and it is here, on this level, that any youth makes or breaks the first half of his life. He thinks he wins his maleness by great accomplishments "out there," but the real dragon battle is a totally interior one. When that battle is won, he can accomplish "out there" and have something to show the world and prove his value. But no amount of "out there" accomplishment can settle the dragon battle, and there are many men of all ages who have accomplished great things and amassed great fortunes but who are still vulnerable to the inner dragon or mother complex.

Ernest Hemingway fought many outer battles—bullfighting in Spain, adventuring in war and at sea—that have made fine literature. But he never conquered the dragon within and when his youth had run out and he had no more strength for "out there," he consented to the mother complex by suicide. It is a certain indication of an unresolved mother complex in a man when he continues adolescent bravado past his midteens. It is a sign of the bad prognosis for American masculinity that the fiction of male bravado is so popular with men long past the time when they should have slain their dragons. Far too many modern men make a hue and cry over maleness in outer form while they are quietly losing their inner dragon battles by default. Tons of sporting equipment and fleets of fast cars are sold to bolster the male image, but these are a sad substitute for that wonderful-terrible moment when a young man slays his dragon and is free from his longing to return to the dependence of boyhood and be taken care of by a mother. One straight answer to a direct question or one good decision will do more to banish the mother complex than all the bolstering of male image that one could buy. But what can you do with a culture that takes the cowboy as its most virile symbol of maleness? Half of that word (*cow*) is feminine; the other half (*boy*) is immature. Why not *bullman?*

A particularly touching example of the mother complex is found in the Grail myth, that great Western repository of instruction on becoming a man. Parsifal, who is to be the hero of the story and attain a vision of the Grail (which will be a great symbol of the mother archetype later in our discussion), begins as the fatherless son of a mother who is determined to prevent him from falling into the nonsense of knighthood, which had earlier cost the life of her husband and other sons. She makes a one-piece homespun garment for Parsifal when he announces he will go out into the world to be a knight like his father. This homespun is Parsifal's mother complex in its symbolic, mythological form. Every young man goes out with his mother complex wrapped about him, which will defeat him as long as he wears it as his relationship with the world. The complex has little to do with his actual mother (though a flesh-and-blood mother can lay the seeds of defeat in her son if she wishes to keep him as her own, or she can give him the freedom and the courage to become a man). If the son adopts this protective garment as his adaptation to the world, he has taken refuge in his mother complex and is alienated from his manhood. No amount of bravado or even intelligence can make a man out of a youth who is clothed in his homespun mother complex.

Just to know that one carries the secret wish for defeat embedded in the mother complex is to be protected from the dragon battle. Not to recognize this portion of one's feminine heritage is to be locked in bravado and the ceaseless battle of proving one's value. Masculinity "out there" is not difficult to achieve when one has fought the dragon battle. That terrible inner battle is totally feminine and is such a baffling struggle for a male. Just to define it is to begin one's freedom.

Most dark moods in a man are his mother complex coming to the surface. It is so strange that a big strong male who could hold his own on any external battlefield can be so easily defeated by a mood. There is the story of a great hero, Tristan, who fought and killed a dragon that was ravaging the countryside. Another man, a false hero (someone trying to resolve his mother complex by trickery or bravado), cuts the tongue out of the dragon and takes it back as proof that he did the heroic deed. The dragon tongue, hidden away in his pouch, drips poison and wounds the usurper-hero so badly by its poison that he loses the power that he pretended he had won. To be anywhere near a dragon is to be endangered by its poison, which attacks a man in that so very vulnerable place—his moods. The mother complex fights in this strange underhanded way that is so puzzling to a male.

Fighting with a feminine element is like fighting with a fog bank. Rough masculinity is completely ineffective; consciousness and clarity are the effective tools.

I remember a midnight ride by bus from the airport to my home. There were six of us in the bus and the conversation drifted around to what kind of car each of us had. One had a Cadillac, another a Jaguar, another a Mercedes, another a BMW. I sat in terror awaiting the moment they would ask me what car I drove. To admit the truth was more than my masculinity could endure. I thought of lying to save face but instead blurted out, "Mine is a paid-for VW." Behind my feeling of inferiority was my fear of my mother complex in the eyes of my peers. It may be argued that the collision between outer values—the list of expensive cars and mine of lesser status—was what made me so uncomfortable. But it was my fear that the mother complex might win the desperate battle within my own psychology that produced the terror.

A young man's insistence on dangerous adventures is a thin disguise for his mother complex. To risk being killed on a motorcycle or to hang precariously on a cliff signals the intrusion of the mother complex masquerading as ultimate maleness. The wish to fail or to die is so strong in a man with a mother complex that he has to expose himself to these regressive experiences frequently to win his battle over them.

The dragon battle always leaves a scar that is a constant reminder all through a man's life that he came near to losing the basic battle of his life—the battle between life and death. Every man wears a scar on the underside of his penis that is a reminder of the time in his fetal life when he was not yet a male. His genitals, remarkably like female organs at this stage of development, were not yet differentiated into a male organ. Masculinity comes sometime after conception in fetal life and sometime after physical maturity in psychological life. The scar is also a reminder that the battle is never completely won and the paralyzing effect of the mother complex can challenge a man anywhere along his life journey. For clarity, the stories speak of a single decisive battle, but in fact it is a battle to be repeated many times.

Suicide is the ultimate defeat by the mother complex. When one kills himself he consents to the great regressive force of the mother complex; she wins the battle, and death prevails.

It is not uncommon for a man to project his mother complex onto an impersonal institution. The university, the church, the club, or the YMCA is often the repository of one's mother complex; one can treat these institutions as places of regression where one can evade life. Many a man finds housing for his mother complex in the university by becoming the perpetual student and remaining in perpetual adolescence. Of course, it is not the institutions themselves that are to blame but one's attitude toward them. To take refuge in an institution is just one of the many disguises of the will to evade life. Exactly the same institution can be a legitimate part of one's life if he has eradicated the mother complex as evasion.

It is interesting to observe the difference between East and West in the way the mother complex touches us and the two different solutions to it.

It is a basic law that the unconscious presents to us the face that we have first presented to it. If the inner world seems hostile or dragonlike, it is always because we have first antagonized it. Our Western way is to take a heroic stance in life, to battle our way past great obstacles to gain the treasure and the fair maiden. This heroic plunge toward what we want sets up the opposition in the unconscious that we call the mother complex. If we want to wrest the treasure from the inner world, that inner world will put up heavy resistance to defeat us and the hero–mother complex battle is defined. Our Western prescription is to battle with all one's might, kill the dragon, and win through to the treasure and the fair maiden.

The East teaches quite a different attitude. In Eastern psychology, if one finds an antagonism going on he is taught to withdraw the cause of the antagonism by meditation, detachment, finding a stillness in his attitude and thus bringing the opposition to a stop. If the antagonistic forces are diminished the battle will stop. The East has described this cessation of antagonism as the Divine Nothing, the Great Void, the Stillness, the Creative Nothing, Nirvana—the still point.

No greater insight into Western psychology can be gained than by contrasting our hero myths and attitudes toward life with their Eastern counterparts.[2] This is not to say that one way is better than the other, and one should be very cautious if he chooses to adopt an Eastern way, since our unconscious structure is not well equipped for this way of nonresistance. But the contrast is instructive from either point of view.

I remember a vivid comment by Richard Morris Bucke[3] on the contrast between the lined and furrowed countenance of Walt Whitman, so much a Western hero, and the

2. See my book *Femininity Lost and Regained* (New York: HarperCollins, 1990) for a comparison of Western and Eastern myths.

3. Richard Morris Bucke, *Cosmic Consciousness* (New York: Dutton, 1969).

timelessness and boyishness of the serene, unlined face of a Hindu sage. Bucke confesses his own preference for the face that had been etched by life and had seen the heroic way.

I think both the Eastern and the Western are noble ways; but both require that one know what he is doing and be highly conscious of the path he has chosen.

Even the mother complex, dark as it is in a young man's life, has its rightful place. Finally, it is she who welcomes him into death and enfolds him in the eternal peace that is her creative side. If a man falls prey to this too soon he has embraced death instead of life and will have a very hard time. But at the right moment, it is the mother complex that brings a man to the culmination—and end—of his life. There is an old myth that portrays man's life as the sun making its way across the heavens every day. He resists the pull of gravity and the seduction of the ocean and makes his masculine way through his creative solar day. But at evening, he loses his energy and descends toward the earth or sea of the mother. Just as she claims him for her own, he produces his phallus at the last instant, mates with her, and thus ensures his rebirth the next morning at sunrise. Anyone living near the western ocean will have seen the sun making his phallus as the distortion of the different densities of air draws the sun into brief fantastic shapes the moment before sunset.

In Egypt a sarcophagus is often painted with the body of the great mother on the bottom and her two arms on the underside of the lid. To be put into one's coffin is to be given back to the enfolding arms of one's mother.

At the high point of his journey, Faust is instructed by Mephistopheles, his shadow, to go to the place of the mothers and insert the key into the tripod he will find there. This is the culmination of Faust's journey and it makes proper use of the mother complex that we have been describing in such dark terms.[4] When a man has fought the dragon battle in his personal life and gained the strength of his manhood—and what a long battle that is!—then he can make that extremely dangerous journey back to the place of the mothers and restore his connection there. This is possible only for a gifted person and then only when he has gained enough masculine strength and clarity to bear this dangerous journey. This is the stuff of genius and not for ordinary men.

I find it most encouraging that every element of one's psychology is useful in the right place. It is only the misplacing

---

4. See my book *Transformation: Understanding the Three Levels of Masculine Consciousness* (San Francisco: HarperSanFrancisco, 1991) for a detailed discussion of this use of the mother complex.

of an element that constitutes wrongness or evil. Even the mother complex is constructive when it is in its correct place.

The Mother Archetype

It is a relief to leave the darkness of the mother complex and explore the lofty realms of the mother archetype. While the mother complex is so dangerous to a young man, the mother archetype is pure gold. This noble realm is the place of mother nature, life, nourishment, support, strength. The mother archetype surrounds us at all times and in every direction. It is the air we breathe, the water, the whole physical universe that supports us. Without the mother archetype we would not live for one second. It is the whole mothering world in its divine essence—reliable, nurturing, benevolent. It is not too much to say that the mother archetype is the feminine half of God.

Probably the two mother manifestations—complex and archetype—are the same entity, different only in the way we relate to them. If one is weak and making that awful regression that is the deadliest enemy of any man, he sees the mothering principle as destructive to him; if he approaches it with strength and meets it as an equal, then it is the whole world of strength and the specifically feminine quality of life and duration.

The task of any young man can be described simply as the art of transforming his mother complex into the mother archetype. To accomplish this is to turn his regressive, complaining qualities into a native security in life and the strength of accomplishment. A man supported by his mother archetype has a wonderful vision of strength and power.

Returning to the story of Parsifal and his homespun garment, we can see his maturing relationship to the Holy Grail, as he succeeds in casting off his mother complex and gaining the power to relate to the Grail, which is the prime symbol of the mother archetype. The story tells us that Parsifal blundered into the Grail Castle in his midteens but could not ask the required question that would have given him entrance to the Grail Castle anytime he wished. Burdened with his homespun garment (mother complex), he is silent and does not have the power to make the Grail experience conscious. It takes him twenty years of life experience to divest himself of his homespun garment so that when he has another chance to see the Grail in the holy procession, he can ask the proper question and gain continuous access to the Grail. This is the mythological description of a young man translating his mother complex into the mother archetype. Few things in a man's life are as rewarding.

Much of a man's experience in the middle third of his lifespan consists of gaining enough consciousness and insight to make the transition from mother's homespun to mature knighthood. Parsifal had to do his duty as a knight, fighting dragons, rescuing fair maidens, raising a siege on a castle—all the things that adulthood requires of one. In modern terminology, a man must "grow up" and get beyond "I, me, mine."[5] A young man must make this transition from complex to archetype before he is capable of doing a man's work, occupying a place in the adult world, or forming any mature relationship. Any fault in this transition is like a chink in his armor that leaves him vulnerable.

The Sister

When a man has set out to conquer his mother complex with all its dragon battles and has learned a little of the majesty of the mother archetype, he is ready to look at what we arrogantly call the "real" world. The first model of

5. See my book *He* for a more detailed description of this process.

femininity he sees—aside from his actual mother, who is probably so misty in his attitudes that she is more myth than fact—is his sister. She represents "reality" to him in feminine form and is his first contact with an actual flesh-and-blood woman whom he can comprehend. She is companion, friend, enigma, trusted confidante, ally, competitor, and his initiation into the mysteries of femininity. Since she is the first woman he is likely to know near his own age, her example determines many of his attitudes toward women for the rest of his life.

The sister is a wonderfully safe world and an initiation into that mysterious realm that is soon to claim so much of a man's attention. Affection and simplicity are the great values of this relationship.

The sister is often the prelude to the anima for a man. She strengthens him and prepares him for the incredible world of anima that is soon to come into his life. To have a good sister image in one's background is to have good preparation for the unfathomable world of courtship and marriage soon to come. The sister is a "trial run" for that great expansion of life that is the world of courtship.

I remember a young man, badly wounded in several levels of his feminine nature, who dreamed that he must first contact his sister before he could cope with "the girl with the sparkling eyes" who was to be his salvation.[6] The dream portrayed his sister as his first contact with a numinous healing world that had nearly been destroyed by a severe mother complex. In the dream the sister appeared only briefly, but she represented a bridge between mother and anima that is absolutely essential to a man. Many a man has his sister to thank for this development in his early life.

It will become more clear in the section on the anima that the sister is the beginning of the numinous world of femininity that has so much power over a man's life. Dr. Jung defines the anima as the intermediary between the conscious personality of a man and the depths of his being, the collective unconscious. This has so much to do with a man's happiness and his sense of value and worth on the face of the earth. His sister is only the introduction to this magical world, but she has much to do with his attitude toward it.

A man is introduced to the magical kingdom of femininity by his sister before that realm is charged with the full power of sexuality and adulthood. A man without a sister or with a negative sister experience does not have a good entrée to the

---

6. See my book *Inner Work: Using Dreams and Active Imagination for Personal Growth* (San Francisco: Harper & Row, 1986) for a description of this remarkable dream.

magical kingdom of femininity. I remember a man who late in his life defended his older sister, who was behaving with something less than dignity, by saying, "Yes, but don't forget—it was she who bought me my first suit [in the Depression years] and taught me to stand tall and have faith in myself." This is a sister's legacy to one man and a fine start in his life.

The sister is easily a positive force in one's life. It is only when the sister image is contaminated by some other level of femininity that it is likely to turn dark or destructive.

We tend to relegate the sister image to a place of simplicity in our lives—a part of the Garden of Eden when things were right. But an examination of the sister image in other cultures reveals it to have startling power and depth!

Incest was forbidden in ancient Egypt with all the same force and finality as in most cultures. A man was to be killed without trial or discussion if he was found in any incestuous situation. But the Pharaoh was obliged to marry his own sister and could have no one else for a wife![7] This is the first clue that brother-sister relationship holds depth unexplored in our culture.

---

7. See my book *Femininity Lost and Regained* for a discussion of this difficult subject.

In Greek mythology there is the story of Mausolus and Artemisia, brother and sister who inherited the kingdom when their father, Hecatomnus, died. They married and ruled the kingdom jointly, making a golden age of peace and beauty. When Mausolus died, his sister made a tomb for him that became the fifth of the seven wonders of the ancient world, the Mausoleum at Halicarnassus. Our word *mausoleum* comes from Mausolus's name. This story tells of a type of brother-sister relationship not often explored in our culture—one characterized by intimacy.

Saint Augustine warned that brother and sister should not marry because the love between them might be too great to bear.[8]

Though it is largely ignored in our time, the brother-sister relationship has depths unfathomed in our attitudes. One has only to read the extraordinary book *My Sister and I* by Nietzsche (said to have been smuggled out of the asylum where Nietzsche was hospitalized for the last years of his life) to see what effect a sister image can have on a sensitive man.[9]

---

8. I am indebted to Betty Smith for this information from Greek mythology and from Saint Augustine.

9. Friedrich Nietzsche, *My Sister and I* (New York: Amok, 1990).

We keep the mystery of young man and woman for the level of man and anima in our cultural structures and mostly ignore the archetypal depths of brother and sister.

The Anima

The anima is, indeed, the world of magic and mysticism. She, who has so much to do with a man's happiness and sense of worth, is almost total mystery. She delights and puzzles and pains a man, and he has so little comprehension of this magic interior world!

In this unfathomable subject, it is best to begin with Dr. Jung's definition of the anima, for it was he who discovered her and named her for this generation. He chose the term *anima* because it is her chief characteristic that she *animates* and gives life. She has been called *la femme inspiritrice,* muse, poetic voice, guide, psychopomp; she has borne the name of Helen (she who launched a thousand ships in ancient Greek lore), Beatrice (immortalized by Dante in the *Comedia Divina*) and Candide, and whatever name is etched into a man's heart as the one who awakened his soul in midadolescence. All virtue and inspiration seem to lie in her gentle hands. She carries a man's soul and is mistress of his inner world. Dr. Jung speaks of her as the intermediary between a man's conscious personality and the depths of his nature, the collective unconscious. She is the queen of all the psychopomps, those intermediaries who keep us in contact with the mysteries and depths of our nature. She is the inspirer, the bearer of poetry, the guide through the underworld, the essence of encouragement (a word meaning "strengthening of the heart"), and, probably deepest of all, she is the carrier of meaning. It is she, with her magic and her interior connection, who bestows meaning and value in a man's life. When a man is in her presence—inwardly in his deepest inner world, or outwardly when he is in the presence of someone to whom he has given this power—the slightest nod of approval or talisman from her hand is enough to give meaning and justification to the whole of his life.

Plato gives a fine description of the search for one's other, his anima. He describes the original human being as a round person, containing both male and female elements. This round one splits into two equal halves when it incarnates, and each half—a complete male or female, vaguely aware that it is incomplete, lacking its original circular form—spends its lifetime searching for its lost other half. This search occurs obviously in its outer form as one devotes so much time and energy to looking for the perfect partner and soul mate; in its inner form, it is a much more diffuse and vague discontent and search for meaning. So much of the vitality of life is invested in these two avenues, and most of the sense of worth and meaning of life comes in this language. To be aware of this search is to be very close to the secret of life.

Men and women have very different experiences in their search, which gives so much of the character we ascribe to masculine and feminine. This awareness is essential in making one's way through the labyrinth of early life with its courtship and the later part of life with its search for meaning. Masculine and feminine are but two sides of the same hunger for completeness and the religious experience of ecstasy and wholeness.

A man's hunger for that numinous experience of femininity that would complete his one-sided masculinity takes him into the realm of softness, warmth, gentleness, which is so intriguing and baffling to him. More than anything else he hungers for validation of his masculine world. Only a feminine value will give this validation. Nothing is so sweet to a man as to find that gift of meaning, the validation of what he is and does. He searches for this completion in the realm of femininity, whether from an actual flesh-and-blood woman or from his own inner feminine nature. The great myths speak of the man doing his exploits and long journeys and pilgrimages—always for the nod of approval or the bestowing of some talisman from his lady fair. Often the lady fair does nothing but wait in her castle while the hero does his great deeds and risks his life in battle for her or for a noble principle that she represents. If one took this literally it would paint a very poor picture of woman's place in the world. But taken inwardly, where it belongs, it portrays the inward-turned feminine half of the man himself, who must tend inner values and defend that half of reality.

Men and women search for such different experiences in each other! He searches for validation, warmth, gentleness to add to his already angular, direct maleness. A man's hunger to be understood is one of the strongest in his whole character. A nod of approval, a talisman, even a word—these are the heart and soul of meaning to him. Countless movies and novels revolve around the hunger of the hero for the approval and validation of his beloved. No journey is too long nor heroic feat too dangerous to undertake in order to fulfill this burning need. Much of the roughness in a man is but a clumsy way of asking for this validation. And a man is so vulnerable to the threat of losing this validation. A flip comment from his lady fair is all it takes to turn triumph into ashes for him. A woman comprehends so little of this mechanism in a man and rarely knows what power she wields over him.

The anima in her inner dimensions in a man obeys the same laws but in a much more subtle form. In this realm a man lives at the mercy of his moods—which are his feminine side lived inwardly—and the nod of approval or the withholding of the flow of life itself by his inner woman has the same effect on him as in its outer form. A man in a bad mood is as incapacitated as one whose outer world has been dashed to pieces by the failure of his outer anima relationship. A man wounded by his lady fair, inner or outer, finds his energy incapacitated, for it is she who is the mistress of his power and strength. A man in a mood is a sundial in moonlight telling the wrong time.

A woman asks very different things of masculinity. Stability, protection, form, order, clarity, freedom are her needs from her man. He so often fails to hear this and blunders about with great plans and rootless visions and thus wounds her terribly by his incomprehension. Men and women are so often like ships passing in the night without seeing or comprehending each other. The night of incomprehension must come to an end if relationships are to gain the dignity and freedom that is our contemporary vision for them.

Each wounds the other mainly by the incomprehension of the mute but desperate needs the other is carrying. To hear the strange, exotic needs of one's companion is pure genius in relationship.

There is a wonderful story of an English lord who went to his solicitor (lawyer) and asked the extraordinary favor of a divorce done as quietly and inconspicuously as possible. The solicitor agreed on the condition that the lord and lady spend one hour with a counselor. The therapist, wise in such ways, found out that the lord had fallen in love with a circus performer, age 21, and could not live his life without her. The lady then burst out with the carefully hidden fact that she had always wanted to be a circus performer but the strict English ways of their station in life had forced her to bury this desire and never give it any place in their long married life. The story ended happily; you can supply the subsequent conversation between the two. Two individuals had starved each other to the point of desperation and found common language only at the last moment. One often sees married couples that have not heard each other on the most tender and important dimensions of life. And, though the language of man and woman is very different, they speak a common tongue. He who has ears to hear . . .

It must be argued that the anima is, finally, a completely interior experience for a man. In our culture he almost invariably projects this quality onto a flesh-and-blood woman, but this does not override the fact that she is a soul quality and essentially has her home in the deepest interior of a man's life. The flesh-and-blood woman has enormous power in a man's life, but the anima is an interior psychic organ for every man. Later we will have to explore the contaminations or overlays every man makes that muddy the clear vision of his soul nature. The anima is so strong that it seems impossible for a man to understand her directly in the first part of his life, and he has to assign her reality to some projection—generally onto a real woman—before he can comprehend the profoundly religious experience she brings to him. To project one's anima onto a real woman is to miss the interior meaning of life and—worse yet—to fail to see his real-life companion in her human dimensions. If a man asks his fiancée or wife to be a goddess, he sets the stage for an inevitable tragedy. She fails to be his goddess and, blinded by his great hunger for the divine feminine, he fails to see her as the human being she is.

There are two great treasures in a man's life: his wife and his interior anima. These are of equal reality, but they have a terrible way of obscuring each other. To differentiate between these two powerful forces in a man's life is an absolute prerequisite for outward relationship and inward meaning.

It is possible to find the anima in "inanimate" objects, but such an arrangement always "animates" that object in a magical way. Witness the young man who endows his car with almost human qualities or bestows mystical qualities on a treasured musical instrument. He may even give it a feminine name. Any treasured pursuit or divinized object is a potential carrier of one's anima. How many women—who always have a better understanding of such things than men—have to stand by and mutely watch their men make a mystery and fetish of something they see through in an instant? Even the most intelligent man is subject to the anima seduction of life, while a woman sees through it immediately. A woman is equally subject to her interior magic by way of her animus, but that is for another book.

As if there were not enough mystery about the anima, she generally comes in double form in a man's life. This seems so indelible a fact that it leaves its imprint in man's behavior anywhere the anima appears. The two anima figures generally represent the light and the dark sides of man's capacity for appreciating the feminine. The light anima is often idealistic, lofty, noble, ascetic; the dark anima is a gypsy, illicit, wildly sensuous, chaotic. How the dual nature of the anima manifests itself may be as simple as the youth dating first a blond, then a brunette in his exploration of the mystery of the anima; or it may be the built-in tragedy of Tristan, unable to relate to either of the two Iseults—one angelic, the other very human—in his life without contaminating one with the other.[10] The double anima is one of the points of greatest suffering in a man's life, and our modern world is far from a solution to it. Various cultures have taken various attitudes toward the double anima. Some cultures allow several wives; others allow concubines; still others condone a wife and a mistress. Our official stance is to marry once and by sheer discipline ignore the other anima possibilities in life, or one may try serial marriages, or ——— ? The possibilities are endless, but none seem very satisfactory. If one brings his best discipline to bear on the subject, his unlived anima is likely to languish and go negative or die and leave the man lifeless in middle age. Or if one follows the current trend and lets his anima rule his life without bringing discipline to her, he probably will fall into the chaos that is so

10. See my book *We: Understanding the Psychology of Romantic Love* (San Francisco: Harper & Row, 1983) for an elaboration on this theme.

common in relationship today. An ideal solution is to marry a woman who bears one of a man's anima images and invest the other in an art or creative endeavor in his outer life. It is one of the large cultural tasks facing us in our age to find a creative solution to the double anima in man.

An African tale portrays the double anima with startling clarity. The story tells of a father who warns his young son that the heavenly woman will come one night and ask to lie beside the son. The father describes the beauty and seductiveness of this heavenly vision and informs the son that he will be dead in the morning if he agrees to the offer of the heavenly woman. The father grows increasingly worried about this danger to his son (perhaps he knew the heavenly woman earlier in his own life?) and moves to a new village so the heavenly woman may not find the son. But when the parents are away, the heavenly woman comes to the son at night and asks to lie beside him. Though he has been warned, the son is so dazzled by the beauty of the maiden that he agrees to let her lie beside him for the night. In the morning the son is dead and the heavenly woman is horrified, since she had no wish to injure the youth. She goes quickly to an old shaman who lives nearby and asks for help. The old shaman comes and after some time builds a huge fire and tosses a lizard into the hottest part of the fire.

He says that anyone who loves the dead youth enough to walk into the fire and retrieve the lizard will return the youth's life to him. The heavenly woman tries but fails; the youth's mother tries but fails; his father tries but fails. The fire is too hot. Then a plain girl from the village who loves the youth but has never let this be known walks into the fire and retrieves the lizard. It is her ordinary human love that has the power to rescue the youth. The boy awakens and we wish that the story might end here in so much happiness. But one more episode remains. The old shaman tells the celebrating village that one more decision remains. He builds the fire again, throws the lizard into the middle of the flames, and informs the boy that he must make a decision. If he retrieves the lizard from the fire (a power he now has), the plain maiden will live and his mother will die. If he leaves the lizard in the fire, the plain maiden will die but his mother will live. The story does not tell us which decision the youth makes but leaves that sacrificial moment for each man to decide in his own life.

The story has great power and tells of the double anima in a man with stark clarity. The heavenly woman is his light anima; the plain girl is his earthly, human capacity for relatedness. The heavenly vision utterly incapacitates a young man for ordinary life, and he can be saved only by the earthly capacity for relationship represented by the plain maiden. Then all of this reverts to the mother, and he has to choose between his mother and his human anima (the ability to create).[11] If he chooses to save his mother but sacrifices the plain maiden, he will be a possible candidate for shaman for the next generation. If he sacrifices his mother and saves the plain maiden, he gains the capacity for an ordinary human life. To fail to make this choice means the loss of both. Later in his life he will be able to recover whichever one was sacrificed at this early point in his life, by building a conscious life that finds the right place and level for all of these elements. All of these choices and experiences come to every young man and present themselves in the particular language of his own unique life.

The Wife

What a relief to find a flesh-and-blood human after trying to comprehend the tremendum of the anima! One's wife is most specifically human. She has her own distinct character,

11. This is a primitive story from Africa, where the heavenly anima and the mother archetype are often indistinguishable.

is refreshingly human, has weight and substance, and is capable of human companionship, which is not characteristic of any other feminine entity. Throughout the very long history of marriage, men have treated wives in such a wide variety of ways! Man has made of his wife a slave, a drudge, chattel, a workhorse, a companion, a heroine, a goddess, a sexual convenience. He has seemed capable of myriad impositions upon her but maddeningly unable to see her for what she actually is—a human being. To relate to one's wife as that specific human being that is her essence, is probably the best compliment one could offer her. How many hundreds of times have I instructed a man, "Go home and listen to your wife for half an hour and find out who she really is!" A revelation awaits such a man.

The worst possible contamination of levels appears in the relationship to one's wife, and probably the worst of one's neurotic structure falls on her. It is our job later to examine these contaminations, but it must be said in this description that man makes the most serious overlays or contaminations with his attitude toward his wife. Few wives feel acknowledged for the person they truly are.

Traditional cultures have all dictated specific forms and structures for relationship to one's wife. Those people in their simple wisdom have understood that the husband-wife relationship is subject to complications that it cannot bear, so they contain it in a strict form for its safekeeping. Our recent explorations in freedom have brought severe dangers into this relationship, and we will have to redefine it very carefully.

The Daughter

The relationship with a daughter is a very human relationship and basically simple if one does it correctly. Care, safety, nurturing, initiation into the human world are the father's gifts to his daughter. It is a fortunate daughter who brings a sense of safety and security into adulthood as her father's gift.

Innocence is a daughter's right in the presence of her father. When the daughter is ready to take her place in the adult world, the old custom is for the father to bestow her upon the man who is to take her into adult relationship. All this sounds archaic and naive now, but it is not a bad representation of father and daughter. We have updated this and sneer at its simplicity; modern women refuse to be "handed around" from one man to another, but some of this structure is worth saving. A man does give his daughter over to another stage of life when she leaves his house. It may be to her husband, to a career, to her own independence, or to the individuality that is a woman's birthright. In any case, the parting gift of strength and safety from a father is one of the greatest gifts a daughter can have.

Simplicity is a good ruler of the exchange between father and daughter. Terrible danger follows if a father oversteps his boundaries and takes his daughter into other realms of his feminine nature. A father-daughter relationship keeps a freshness and natural delight if he has lived out the other aspects of his femininity on correct levels.

Sophia

Sophia is a depth of femininity not often experienced by a man. Only he who has earned the right of depth has access to this goddess. She is vast, impersonal, always with an aura of ancientness about her. She is the carrier of the *luminae natura,* that specific wisdom found only in earth or lunar representation. The sun gives the solar masculine wisdom and light, but it is the moon or the lamp fed by the oil of the earth that gives the soft, human, warming light of Sophia. She is a summation of all the feminine virtues and appears only to the man who is capable of such a synthesis without contaminating them into an indistinguishable blur.

When a man comes to that time in his life when synthesis is required of him, he can depend on the genius of Sophia.

Alchemy—that treasure house of psychological insight that is so often mistaken for the early attempts at chemistry—traces out the steps of synthesis in poetic language. One first encounters the Nigredo, the darkness, depression, despair of life. When he has surmounted that, he comes to the Albedo, the brightness and exhilaration of life. Then he finds the Rubedo, the redness of life, which is the passion, accomplishment, "red-bloodedness." Last is the Citrino, the goldenness of life. This is insight, asceticism, wisdom, inspiration. When he has accomplished these four stages he has the right to the Pavanes (the peacock's tail), which has all the colors complementing each other in sublime pattern. If he does it badly, he gets a mud-brown, which is the mixture of all the colors of the rainbow. If he does it well, he has the splendor of life as his reward. Sophia is the ruler of this "rightness."

Sophia is the reconciler, she who softens the harsh edges of masculine form and differentiation and gives it a human and earthborn touch. She has enough of shadow and darkness in her to blur slightly the harsh dictum of masculinity. Things are earth-possible in her light and can be lived. Zeus by himself, in his solar splendor, is too much to endure; but with the mediating softness of Sophia, Olympus comes to its true glory. Knowledge by itself is too harsh for human endurance; lunar femininity by itself is hopelessly diffuse and imprecise. But Sophia, in her timeless wisdom, finds a light that is not harsh and provides a consciousness admirably suited for human life.

The Hetaira

Hetaira is the Greek term for a particular kind of woman—or that aspect of all women—who is a companion, an intellectual partner, a carrier of grace and beauty, a source of inspiration. All women have the hetaira capacity in their natures, and in some it is so strong as to dominate their personality structure. It is no less powerful for us in our own modern times, but we have virtually no terminology for it and little differentiation of this powerful aspect of woman. In ancient Greece, hetaira women would be hired or invited to a party to provide the grace and beauty that can come only from such a woman. She would be well educated, conversant with many timely subjects of conversation, gifted in her ability to bring a particular charm to a gathering, which is one of the most valuable contributions anyone can bring to a group. She would be immaculately dressed, well versed in courtesy and grace, the bearer of delight and warmth. She was never a prostitute and one would no more touch a hetaira woman than the queen of the realm. She was femininity raised to its highest dignity and grace.

I will never forget the woman who came to me in a flood of tears after a lecture on feminine typology, sobbing out her gratitude; "I am not a slut," she said, "I am a hetaira woman!" Our lack of differentiation and poverty-stricken language in feeling terms had given her a very poor self-image when she was capable of some of the finest feminine expression known to man. Many women with a finely developed hetaira quality lead miserable lives—both in their own self-depreciation and in the eyes of other people. We have no forms for the expression of the hetaira quality and it either lives guiltily in disguised form or dies under the heavy hand of repression.

Hetaira women often feel used and that their personal lives have been utterly disregarded. They often do not marry, since the hetaira quality has a great impersonality about it and does not lead to ordinary or family relationship. It is not uncommon for a hetaira woman to come near the end of her life without having accomplished the ordinary feminine tasks. "I feel like a squeezed lime," was one woman's comment. Her hetaira quality gives her the highest value to others but also endangers her personal feminine life.

The geisha still survives in Japan, giving form to the hetaira woman in that stylized culture. Unfortunately, the geisha has lost much of her dignity in modern Japan and is often thought of as an expensive prostitute. But her origins are in that graceful hetaira quality that ancient Greece named and honored.

No Western form exists for her that I am aware of.

I knew a woman long years ago who was a natural hetaira. I went occasionally to her modest apartment just to feast on the grace that she could provide. The careful appointments of her rooms spoke of dignity; her manner drew the best out of me. A cup of tea from her hand was mythology set into motion. My intelligence rose in her presence and I knew things I had not known before entering her aura. I would put forth some new idea that had just come to me, inspired by her presence, and she would raise one eyebrow and say, "Oh." This inspired me still further and more intelligence would come forth from me. She would raise the other eyebrow and give validity to what I had said. I was in seventh heaven!

It would be easy to say that this was a disguised love affair going on under the camouflage of tea and cakes; but I think the relationship had a quality sufficiently unique to deserve its own terminology. The Greeks also thought so and gave the honored term *hetaira* to such women. The Japanese honor her as geisha. We ignore her and lose one of the most precious feminine values known to man.

Friendship

It is strange that friendship between a man and a woman brings some unexpected difficulty. At first glance one would guess that friendship is an easy, uncomplicated matter, a kind of natural haven of warmth and safety. But friendship between a man and a woman is possible only if the preceding man-femininity relationships are mature. Otherwise a man is certain to fall into one of the more primitive modes of relationship with a woman, and the friendship will prove to be one of these primitive exchanges in disguise. Only a mature man is capable of friendship with a woman.

If he has that maturity, a most gentle and tender exchange is possible with a woman. Some of the loveliest moments of one's life lie within this province. There is a grace, dignity, beauty, tranquillity possible between a man and a woman within the structure of friendship that is rarely equaled in any other dimension of life. Fortunate are two people who know this kind of exchange.

Friendship requires leisure. This fine cultural form cannot survive without the time and leisure that are its lifeblood. I love the East Indian custom of standing next to someone in silence, probably just a step in back of him, if you wish to make friends with him. Silence, waiting, time, respect for another's space—these are the elements of friendship.

Chinese culture has a gentle way of talking about friendship: their proverb is that the fifth cup of tea between friends is the best. Tea was made in old China simply by pouring hot water over loose tea leaves in a cup. The explanation of the proverb is that when friends meet, busy and tense from the outside world, the first cup of tea is drunk hastily and without much grace. The second pouring of water requires a longer time to steep the leaves. This is better. The third cup requires still more time. The fifth cup stands for an appreciable length of time before the tea is of the required strength. It is this fifth cup that becomes the symbol of friendship at its best. Even an introverted Chinese person needs the quiet passage of time, measured in cups of tea, to define the deepest friendship. There may be a subtle Chinese hint at another dimension in the symbol of the fifth cup of tea; our word *quintessence,* meaning whole or total, derives from "fifth essence." Wholeness requires time.

Homoerotic Relationships

With the first move into the nebulous land of homoerotic relationships we are hampered by lack of terminology. We will have to improvise and evolve our own language, for it is unknown territory. Never is English so clumsy or inadequate as in surveying relatedness, a faculty of femininity. No wonder we suffer so much in relationship and are the loneliest people in history.

The term *homoerotic* derives from the Greek god Eros. The important clue from that derivation is that Eros pointed his arrows at the heart of his victim, not at the genitals. So the term *homoerotic* will be used in this discussion as being apart from sexual exchange. Homosexuality is the specifically sexual connection between two persons of the same sex.

The homoerotic faculty of a man is the art of relating to the opposite polarity, the femininity, of another man. There can be a specific exchange of feeling between two men with unique characteristics not found in any other relationships.

A closeness that is not based on sexuality is one of the finest and most subtle aspects of relationship. Our culture tends to put this under the general heading of homosexuality; but this closeness is sufficiently specific to warrant its own terminology—terminology we will have to invent or recover since homoerotic relationship has been given no official place in our society. Slang terms have partly filled the gap, and we make uneasy use of *buddy,* or *sidekick,* or the Australian *mate,* for our homoerotic attachments. Locker-room banter warily edges around affection and camaraderie and shies away from anything that looks like homosexuality.

Every man weaves his way through the verbal minefields of feeling and shares time and affection with his buddy, being very careful not to blunder on the taboos of our feeling-poor language. Feeling between men is mostly disguised under towel snapping, rough talk, bravado, showing off, and casualness.

But what is underneath this powerful man-to-man or woman-to-woman exchange?

One language possibility is to call this a subdivision of homosexuality and group it with those characteristics that are getting so much publicity now. But I think the homoerotic capacity is a valid entity in its own right and deserves its own terminology and distinctness.

India's greatest gift to me was the opening of a vivid, colorful world of homoerotic capacities that burst into my life like a revelation. What a joy to find warmth and devotion and sensitivity in such a stable form! I saw man-to-man, woman-to-woman relationships give much warmth and stability to Hindu life. It was quickly evident that much of their happiness springs from this faculty. I jealously watched as my Hindu friends reaped a whole world of security, happiness, delight from their man-to-man relationships. They were easy, uncomplicated, warm, secure in a way I had not witnessed before. I found a gold mine of relationship I had never known before. To my delight, I found I had the capacity for this and could fit into that way of life as quickly as I could dislodge my Western collective fear of the homoerotic world. I promptly had a dream after my first India trip where I saw Queen Victoria as a dead tree stump that I was removing with a bulldozer. I quickly learned that all people have the native capacity for homoerotic relationship, and we have been missing a rich aspect of life in our Western world. Truly, we have sold our birthright—from a feeling point of view—for a mess of potage. We have gained much in exchange that I refuse to give up, but that gain has cost us some of the inner gold of same-sex relationship.

It is the Hindu way of life for a youth to be married twice in his life, first to his buddy, then to his wife. I have an almost irresistible urge to drop this whole subject and run from it at this point, since I have no terminology or vocabulary for it. Marriage? To a man? Our semantic structures don't allow us such thoughts. Then where are the verbal forms that will serve us? They don't exist, and we are denied some of the warmest and most strengthening exchanges of which man is capable.

A Hindu youth gravitates to a companion in his childhood, and that bonding is noted and honored by his community. If one of the boys falls into trouble, the other automatically devotes himself to finding or caring for his buddy. If one dishonors himself, it laps over instantly upon the other. There is a true identity or bonding between the two that lasts for a whole lifetime. This bond is very deep and implies many facets of relatedness not often known to a Westerner. Parallels are to be found in American Indian tribal patterns.

At about age 16 a youth is married to a woman of his own age, and this second marriage is equally bonding for life. A Hindu friend of mine was married, a bit later in age than is traditional, and waited for the ceremony until I could be there with him. He had appointed me as his buddy (where is the terminology adequate to convey such things?) and naturally drew me into the profound experience of his marriage ceremony. Two years later I was in India again visiting my friend and admiring his firstborn. Many people pointed out the fact that the child was lighter in color than either parent and had an immediate explanation. "It is Robert's influence." Few Westerners can escape the uneasiness of a bad joke in this, but no traditional Hindu has any difficulty accepting the fact that my life was inextricably bound up with my friend's. My pocketbook was common property between us, my needs were his needs, we shared many attitudes in common (though I had some difficulty with this since I am much more an individual in my upbringing than he is), and it followed without any question that my light skin was part of our mutual character. Are my friends in America talking about the same thing when they comment on the effect India has had on me?

What happens to his buddy when a man marries and begins his family? His buddy is having a parallel experience, and the two aid and companion each other in every aspect of life. One spends much of his time with his buddy and has a particular kind of affection and camaraderie that is highly stable. I was often astonished at seeing how much safety and security there is in a Hindu life when one is strengthened from both sides of one's nature. One has both his buddy and his wife to help him deal with the vulnerability of life, something we lack very sorely in our Western ways.

Hindu women make the same kinds of bonding and have the same strength in back of them.

There are parallels in our Western world to the Hindu genius for homoerotic relatedness, but we have to reach far back in our history for unselfconscious examples. The Old Testament has many examples of pairs of friends whose stability and closeness were exemplary. David and Jonathan, Christ and John the Evangelist are examples.

An American Indian example of homoerotic nature may be found in the Blackfoot tribe:

> There was another and even closer relationship between boys of the same band, that of partners. Two boys of about the same age became close companions. They played together as children, helped each other in courting girls, went to war together, and offered advice and assistance to each other whenever it might be needed. If a young man was

> wounded in battle, his partner risked his life to carry him to safety and stayed behind the rest of the war party until the disabled man was able to be helped home. In many instances, this close friendship and mutual assistance between partners continued through the rest of their lives.[12]

The Gemini twins are a Greek example of the close ties of two men. The tale goes that Leda was courted by Zeus, who took on the form of a swan and made himself known to her in this disguise. He made her pregnant on the same night that she conceived with her mortal husband. She bore two sets of identical twins, later called the Dioscuri. One set, fathered by Zeus, was Pollux and Clytemnestra. The other set, humanly fathered, was Castor and Helen.

Castor and Pollux went through many heroic adventures together as buddies, and Castor, the mortal one of the pair, was killed. Pollux was devastated by the loss of his companion and refused any activity in the world because of his

---

12. From an article by Mitchell Walker in *Spring,* 1976, a publication of the New York Analytical Psychology Society. Dr. Walker gives his source as J. Ewers, *The Blackfoot* (Norman: University of Oklahoma, 1958), p. 105.

mourning. Zeus offered immortality to Pollux, his son, but Pollux refused since he could not live without his human companion, Castor. So Zeus allowed the two to live with the gods and in the underworld on alternate days. This proved to be so painful that Zeus finally gave them both immortality because of their devotion to each other and raised them to the sky as Gemini, the twins. They embrace in the sky forever, reminding humankind of the nobility of his homoerotic capacity.

This is the Greek imagery for the close relationship between two of the same sex. They are constant companions from earliest childhood and represent the divine and human interplay of every relationship of this kind. Much of the nobility of human character is developed in the matrix of such relationships. A man can discover some of the best of his nature in this exchange, in which human and divine inform each other in a powerful and creative symbiosis.

PART TWO:

Contamination of the Feminine Elements

While every encounter with femininity is correct and fruitful, mixing the forms of femininity makes more trouble for a man than any other single element of his life. It is our task now to see what happens when these feminine forms, each pure genius in its own right, become dark and problematic when indiscriminately mixed. True, probably a man will have to experience all of these forms, but he need not struggle with them in the muddled form that most men experience.

We will explore the specific contaminations that frequently occur in a modern man's life. These contaminations have extremely serious consequences and the information to avoid them is lifeblood to any man.

The Mother Mixed with Other Feminine Forms

The contaminations of one's mother image with other feminine elements—both inner and outer—are the most difficult of all to cope with. The worst of these is the overlay of the mother and the mother complex.

It is extremely rare to find a man who has not muddled his mother and his mother complex into a painful mess. This is so common that it is almost every young man's experience. The most cursory look at the subject will show the chief difficulty of the overlap of these two elements. One is outer, the actual human being who is his mother; and the other is inner, the backward pull, the defeatism and regressive tendency that is interior in every man. If one mixes these he is certain to blame his mother for that inner struggle, the dragon battle of mythology, that rages in his inner world during his adolescence and early youth. Acrimonious battles spring up over nothing between mother and son if this mixture takes place. He is certain to accuse his mother of interfering in his life—and then only a moment later complain because she has not done something for him. The young man must fight his dragon (his mother complex) or he will not tear himself loose from the Garden of Eden of his youth and become a man. Primitive societies have elaborate puberty initiation ceremonies to aid the youth in this. They always exclude women, especially the youth's mother, since she would remind him of the garden paradise that he has to relinquish in order to enter the man's world. The puberty ceremonies are the specific act of leaving the mother world, especially the mother complex, and entering the adult male world. Nothing must be present that would remind the boy-becoming-a-man of the world he is leaving.

In our culture a youth almost always fights his mother (or mother substitute) instead of fighting his interior dragon. I have been party to some wonderful conversations between mother and son in which we have explored the difference between dragon slaying and mother accusing. When one is clear about what he is fighting, the battle becomes much easier. One can dragon-slay without being rude to his mother. It is generally true that a youth cannot be civil to his mother (or the world of the mothers, wherever that may be for him) until he has finished his dragon battle. That is to say, one can make peace with his mother (no matter how saintly she may have been) only when he no longer projects his mother complex onto her.

Many men in our culture are permanently stuck in this contamination, and they are constantly fighting a mother.

What a variety of forms there are! A man's own mother only begins the long list. The poor waitress in the restaurant who elicits a man's rage because she brought the wrong order, the woman office manager, the woman traffic officer, the Republican Party, and the mother in a thousand other disguises incur the wrath of the man who has not made this differentiation between inner complex and outer form.

Dr. Jung once said that any patient who comes to a therapist is either 21 or 45 years old, no matter what his chronological age may be. The entry into life—the 21 year old's dragon battle—occupies the first part of a male life. The relinquishing of material life and the preparation for the life of the spirit is the task of the 45 year old and occupies him for his later years. These two passages are the most important of a man's psychological development, but we are poorly educated in their accomplishment.

A friend noted that the only transition ceremonies we have left in our culture are earning the driver's license at 16 and beginning to draw social security at 65. These are very thin aids to the great transitions that these two stages of life represent.[1]

---

1. I am indebted to Gertrud Mueller Nelson for this quote.

America is now producing a new variation of this in which a man has both of these tasks screaming at him from the unconscious at age 50. If a man has not made his 21 year old's rite of passage, it will dominate him for the rest of his life. When this overlaps with his 45 year old's passage, he has a nearly insoluble muddle. He will try to be both adolescent and mature man at the same time. It is not possible for a man to make the sacrifice required at age 45 if he has not firmly grasped life in his two strong hands at age 21. One cannot sacrifice that which he has never had.

One has only to look at the face and the clothing of any man passing on the street to see where he is in these rites of passage. A 50-year-old face atop a body dressed as an adolescent is a frightening sight.

Colin Turnbull, in his charming book *The Human Cycle,*[2] tells of arriving in India in his late 20s and stumbling, ill with malaria, into a *gurukula,* a traditional Indian school in the Himalayas for bringing a youth through his transition from boyhood to manhood. Its students were 14-year-olds. Since Turnbull had never made this transition (he explains that his English prep school and Cambridge University had

---

2. Colin M. Turnbull, *The Human Cycle* (New York: Simon & Schuster, 1983).

done none of this for him), he began again and recapitulated his early teens in the Indian school. The delight and joy of this experience suffuses every page of his book.

Most of us are not so lucky as to stumble onto a *gurukula* in the Himalayas. Instead, we have to go through that long struggle that is portrayed in all of our myths as the young man fighting his dragon battle and attaining manhood with little help from our customs or modern conventions.

It can easily happen that one's own mother, that specific human being, can be confused with the mother archetype, the bounty of nature and the great cornucopia of all that is good in life. A person thus confused will spend his lifetime comparing a present event with "what Mother would have done." He makes the image of his mother—be she alive or dead—into the touchstone of every experience that comes to him. He will quote his mother or use her as example for many events during the rest of his life. *She* is the criterion by which he judges all value.

What wife has not suffered from her husband's telling her that his mother used to make the apple pie in a different way?

Confusing the mother and the anima is a very serious problem, and the ambiguity of the anima in a man's life allows him many mistakes in this area.

If a man has a disturbed relationship with his actual human mother, it is very easy for him to contaminate his anima, that life-giving interior femininity, with his mother's demands and expectations. A mother-hungry man (and that hunger can dominate a man for his whole lifetime if he has been inadequately mothered) can have the mother image stamped on his life expectations in areas one would not dream of. A mother-hungry man can find himself facing mother in the form of the university he attends, the corporation he works for, the church he attends, the political party he espouses, his nation (we speak of the mother country; German is the only tongue I know of that refers to its homeland as the fatherland), his boat (all boats are *she*) and the ubiquitous term *bitch,* which escapes from a man when he is angry at something that has not gone the way he wishes. These are contaminations of the mother image that can creep into the farthest corners of a man's character.

The contamination of mother and anima is particularly destructive. If a man suffers this muddling, he will have the characteristics of his own personal mother imprinted on every life-giving feeling of his experience. The anima is not exactly feeling in a man's life, but in our paucity of terminology for such things, feeling is the closest common term we have for this important dimension of a man's life. To have every feeling value of one's life overlaid by his mother is to be severely wounded.

The mother-anima overlap sets a man to searching for his personal mother in every idealistic or artistic venture he makes. The anima—she who gives meaning and spiritual depth to a man's life—is the single most important element in his happiness. To have an element as important as this in a man's psychology contaminated by a personal image of mother is to have most of his creative ability incapacitated.

The confusion of mother and wife is so common that it is grist for the mill of cartoonists and joke makers the world over.

Sad is the poor wife who lives in the shadow of her mother-in-law if her husband's mother identification is strong. Living in the shadow of the person of her husband's mother would not be too difficult, but if she lives in the shadow of her husband's mother image, the wife is helpless. Many men never marry in reality but only find their mother in a younger form in the person of their wife. If his wife is in tears at the thought of her mother-in-law's visit, it is probably a comment on the degree to which her husband is mother-identified.

A man only infrequently confuses his mother and his daughter. It is a rare household where a man asks mothering of his daughter, though it is not unknown. If the wife has died or is absent, a man may ask a grown daughter to be his mother. Traditional English households sometimes ask one daughter to stay in the family home to take care of the father if the mother is dead. This is a death sentence to the daughter and demands the complete negation of her own feminine life if she has this burden put upon her. She is unlikely to marry and there is great pressure on her to give up her life to the mother-daughter overlay.

Mother and Sophia are frequently mixed. A man can easily deify his mother and treat her like Sophia. If this is the case, his mother will be the criterion and the embodiment of all wisdom for the rest of his life. This is especially prominent in men who had a very wise or powerful woman as mother. Her ideas, insights, tastes will dominate his life if he has not made the necessary differentiation between his personal mother and the goddess of wisdom. This is often a happy state of affairs but basically is not productive since the man's own femininity has no chance to express itself. Neither will he allow any living woman in his life to have any chance of creativity. A woman in a mother-dominated man's household has little chance to develop her own femininity. It is only from the deep springs of one's own femininity that true creation can take place. And it is only a man of clarity in this regard who can allow his wife or any other woman near him to be creative. A fine mother can help a man on his way, but he must finally put her aside if he is to find his own feminine wellspring. God willing, a wise mother will know this of her son and aid him in this transition. Sad is the man whose mother demands to be queen of his life permanently.

The overlay of mother and friendship is a happy one if a man has done the necessary conscious work and is able to sustain a friendship with a woman. This takes the most careful conscious work but is very fine when it is of good quality. Abraham Lincoln spoke of this kind of relationship with his stepmother, who played such a deep role in his development. It is a wise man and an equally wise mother who can sustain friendship between them.

Mother Complex Contaminations

The darkest qualities appear in a man's life in connection with his mother complex. Though this regressive quality that resides in the bottom of every man's heart has its place, more trouble springs from it than from any other part of a man's interior life. Much of what is observed in ordinary psychological discussion as the mother complex and attributed to the man's relationship to his mother is actually his interior mother complex. Mothers are often blamed for what truly belongs to a man's mother complex. His mother may have contributed to this interior quality, but it is entirely separate from the actual woman who was his mother. The mother complex is the regressive tendency in a man, the wish to retreat and go back to an earlier stage of development where he was safe. Nothing is as dangerous to a man as an unresolved mother complex. Skid row or a drug-and-alcohol rehabilitation center lies not far ahead for a man with a heavy mother complex. Let us examine some of the possible contaminations of the unresolved mother complex.

Examples of men who suffer from a muddling of the mother complex and the mother archetype are to be seen everywhere. When the very central vitality of a man has been damaged or restricted, it is generally because his mother complex—that regressive demand in him—has overpowered his mother archetype, the lifespring of his being. Such people complain endlessly that life has given them a bum deal or that things have been no good or that the cards are stacked against them. Careful examination shows that their will to fail has simply overcome their will to live. The casualties of the mother complex are legion.

Muddling of the mother complex and the anima is very serious and fairly common. If a man projects the deadening character of his mother complex onto his anima, no creativity or brightness is possible in his life. His anima—that bright, animating interior quality—is suffocated by the heavy weight of his will to regress and his basic pessimism. Again, the dragon battle of liberation is the only cure for such a person.

Mythology offers many stories in many languages of the man who must rescue a fair maiden from the imprisonment of a dragon before he can win her and go off with her to "live happily ever after." This is mythological language speaking of freeing one's anima from the clutches of the mother complex and earning the right to proceed with life.

So much of the bravado and bantam-rooster conduct of a young man is the surfacing of the unconscious battle between his mother complex and his anima. When a young man is compelled to play Tarzan and is constantly showing off his strength or skill, he is unwittingly informing the world that he is in the grips of this terrible dragon battle of retrieving his individuality from the dungeon of his mother complex. Most such displays require an admiring fair maiden as audience, which is saying in the simplest terms that he is hoping to escape from the darkness of his mother complex and instill that energy into his anima, she who will animate his life and give him a place in the fully developed male world. The stake in this competition is life itself.

Many stadium events are portrayals of this primordial battle. Bullfighting in Spain, football in America, soccer matches around the world—all of these are arrangements wherein a young man is assigned the hero role and battles the dragon. These may be powerful symbols of what men must do inwardly, but they must leave the spectator role before they can engage in their own dragon battles.

It is a very sad household where a man has fixed his unresolved mother complex on his wife. That poor woman can do nothing right. She is stymied at every move she makes, and she battles against the overwhelming pessimism and destruction of her husband's regressive inclinations. Few women can stand up under the destructive weight of such a man and they either leave the marriage or collapse under the overwhelming despair of such an atmosphere and become a victim of the man's dragon. The mother complex dragon can destroy not only the man himself but any woman who is close to him.

Again, it is the heroic dragon battle of mythology that can save a man from this dark fate.

Muddling the mother complex and the daughter is not a common difficulty but if it does occur in a man, his daughter will proceed into her adulthood with the heavy weight of her father's mistrust and fears on her shoulders. Her father's attitude toward anything feminine will be a part in her own world view and she may be burdened with darkness and pessimism from her father's faulty attitude. One thinks of the biblical injunction: "The sins of a man shall be visited unto the third and the fourth generation." If one construes the word *sin* in this case as the faulty attitude of the man, the biblical phrase has ever-present meaning.

A man with an unresolved mother complex will have little access to Sophia, the goddess of wisdom. That sublime philosophical view of life that is such a treasure in the later part of a man's life will be obscured by the pessimism and destructiveness of his mother complex. Not even the goddess of wisdom herself can stand up under the dissolving effect of the mother complex.

It follows without much examination that friendship with women is impossible in the presence of an unresolved mother complex. The delight, joy, companionship of friendship has no chance in the regressive and destructive atmosphere of the mother complex.

One often senses the death of some fine potential when a man and a woman meet if the mother complex colors the atmosphere. When two people meet, it takes only a few seconds for the mother complex to make an awkward silence of a bright possibility. Then the two people begin searching for some acceptable way to get out of this tense meeting. What might have been a happy discovery of two personalities can be negated in an astonishingly short time by the mother complex. Dr. Jung has said that a contaminated unconscious can lie between two people or in a group like a layer of poisoned fog. All creativity comes to a rapid halt.

Contaminations

In examination of the mother archetype one finds so much joy and brightness that it is hard to find fault with any of its combinations. But on closer examination it is clear that contaminations are as serious in this sphere of life as in any other. The mother archetype is pure gold in its own right; but that pure gold can be negated and made inoperative if it is muddled with other qualities in a way that is limiting to the divinity of the mother archetype.

A man frequently asks the anima to play the role of mother archetype for him. As we have seen, the anima is at her best when she is reserved for the connecting link between the personality and the deep aspects of the collective unconscious. It is she who makes poets and seers and idealists of us all. If a man brings a mother quality into this—even the golden quality of the mother archetype—he is likely to contaminate his most creative faculties with some mother quality, which is not a fruitful combination. Keeping the anima and the mother archetype separate takes the most careful differentiation, one that is not commonly observed in our culture. The Virgin Mary, that sublime carrier of the mother archetype, is also called our spiritual mother. At the same time she is called the epitome of beauty and grace of a young woman, the anima. Perhaps this is not an unhappy blending, but I think a man would serve both anima and mother archetype best if he did not overlap the two.

I cannot forget an early experiment of my own to find greater clarity for my anima–mother archetype. I grew up a

Protestant but have always had a warm attraction to Catholic symbolism. At a crisis in my life I decided I would pour out my heart to the Virgin Mary and see if I could connect with that fount of grace and compassion. I chose the loveliest Catholic church in Los Angeles—a copy of a magnificent building in Seville, Spain, famous for its fine sculptures—and searched out in a quiet moment the exquisitely lovely statue of the virgin. When no one else was in the building I was on my knees pouring out my heart to the virgin. This was going well until I noticed that the halo around her head was a lighted neon tube. This broke some mystical trust in me and I walked out of the building, never again to entrust my soul to a visible image. Perhaps some overlay of levels broke the spell and I could not entrust myself to that expression of faith.

It is commonplace that a man can superimpose the mother archetype upon his wife. If they are simple enough people the marriage can survive, but in any case the projection is a heavy weight on the wife. It is no small task to be the carrier of the bounty of God for a man, and it is too much for any but the simplest people. If a man asks his wife to be the carrier of this feminine bounty and richness he generally asks too much of her, and she escapes from the burden in one way or another. I knew one woman whose husband asked her to be everything high and noble for him. After two or three years of this she went off to an affair with a reprobate. Her comment to me was "That will show him I am not a saint!"

No one likes to be a saint for another; no matter how attractive it may seem at first, it is an insuperable burden.

The combination of mother archetype and friendship offers rich possibilities. He who is capable of friendship with a woman and has earned the right to it often gains much of the beauty of the mother archetype from his friend. There can be a flow of grace, beauty, and insight between two such people that is most rewarding. But even here, one can make the argument that the best is possible only if one is aware of the two levels of exchange going on.

India offers many examples of this combination of faculties. The tenderest friendships exist between a man and an older woman. The mother complex in India seems not so strong and leaves room for more constructive mothering relationships. In India, a man is more deeply mothered in his childhood than in any other culture I know and arrives in adulthood with a minimum of negativity from the mother complex.

Because an Indian man has an easier relationship with the mother archetype than in our Western culture, he frequently has a woman in his environment who takes on the mother archetype for him. He finds a great strength and inspiration from this. He often calls her Mother, and the environment of India gives support to the best of this exchange.

Anima Contaminations

Traditionally, a man spends a month (it is called a honeymoon because it is sweet for the length of a moon) of idyllic bliss with his new wife, then begins the reality process of discovering that his wife is not his anima and is not exactly carrying his expectations of woman. To discover that one's wife is not one's anima (indeed, one may have married someone quite opposite to one's expectations!) is the beginning of relationship. Anything preceding was projection unless both were unusually conscious of the fine art of relating.

To contaminate one's wife with his anima expectations is an error that is commonplace in our world. What woman has not had to inform her husband that she is a person, not an embodiment of his expectations?

So much of the twentieth-century rebellion of woman consists of her instinctive refusal to be the carrier of man's anima. To be human in her own right—not just the carrier of man's expectations of woman—is one of the great liberations of our time. One result of this is that man must learn to carry his own feminine side and take interior responsibility for it. Then, and probably only then, he can see woman for the wonderful creature that she truly is.[3]

The anima and the daughter is so explosive a combination that little has been said about it until recently. When the taboo was lifted, a flood of women spoke out about being molested, physically or psychologically, by their fathers in childhood. A man's anima, especially for Westerners, with its habitual overlap into his sexual realm, has absolutely no business being projected onto a daughter. Little can destroy a daughter so quickly as anima attention—criminal if it is overt, damaging if it is subtle—from her father. If a young girl learns her intimate sexual courtship attitudes from her father she is robbed of a father image and introduced to an incestuous way of life that is horribly damaging.

---

3. See my book *We* for a further discussion of the role of anima in our Western culture.

What are the statistics now of how many women were molested in childhood by their father? The number is horrifying and speaks very badly of our lack of differentiation in the feminine aspects of a man. No man with even rudimentary understanding of the several feminine elements in his personality would bring anima to his daughter. But that understanding is rare, judging from the statistics on the mistreatment of children. Of all the contaminations a human is capable of, this is one of the worst.

Mystical poetry often speaks in the language of a love affair between the penitent and the goddess of wisdom. Perhaps the pairing of anima and Sophia is a legitimate one, but the result would be better if a man were very clear about the difference of levels of the two. Since Sophia is a goddess, she allows no intimacy with a man's personal structure. Since a man relating to Sophia is consorting with a goddess, he must leave the personal dimensions of his life behind. If he brings his anima into his exchange with Sophia, he contaminates his heavenly vision with personal issues.

The heavenly connection—the genius of Sophia—is quickly broken if a man personalizes it. An example of this would be a highly intelligent scientist or inventor who gave us something of great value from his genius. If he were to grow vain or inflated over this, it would be a contamination of two disparate elements—the genius in the depths of his being and his very personal demands.

Semele, the mother of Dionysus, asked something personal of her consort, Zeus, and was instantly incinerated for her error. This story is an excellent example of what happens to a mortal when he or she brings personal elements into the divine realm.

Anima-Sophia contamination is not common with men since very few ever get into any kind of relationship with the heavenly elements. But if one is sufficiently intelligent to have contact with the gods and goddesses, he must use his best wisdom to avoid this contamination. So many of the dark stories about highly intelligent men who make some stupid use of their power are fresh retellings of this age-old story in our modern language.

Friendship between a man and a woman is one of the most rewarding exchanges we can make. A gentle, respectful, intelligent relationship between the two constellates the best in each. A spiritual symbiosis as deep as their potential physical relationship can follow. But a man will often destroy the possibility of friendship with a woman by introducing his anima into the exchange, turning it into a courtship.

Every woman who looks at a man as potential friend carries the fear that the exchange may turn into a courtship or a rape. She fears investing her best femininity in the new friendship since our language and customs make inadequate differentiation among the several feminine possibilities that a man contains. Is he flirting? Or courting? Or dominating? Or is he capable of the friendship that would give her a safe companion? A woman would be so relieved if she could know that a man has these possibilities clearly sorted out. But in our culture they are often in such a tangled confusion that she is not sure what to expect from the man.

A true offer of friendship between a man and a woman is a great carrier of happiness. But a tangle of various elements, most good in their own right, leads to much suffering.

Wife Contaminations

Wife and daughter is the same terrible contamination as anima and daughter but made worse by the fact that it is more easily exteriorized. One of the strongest taboos in all societies is against a man's making a wife of his daughter. As described before, human wreckage invariably results from this contamination.

Overlaying wife and Sophia seldom occurs, but a few examples of it seem rewarding. A husband and wife sometimes collaborate on some mutual research or creative project in their later years. The Durants, husband and wife, gave a profound work of art to the world in their history of civilization. This was a product of a husband-and-wife team working in the realm of wisdom. Still, one hopes they were sufficiently conscious to avoid the negative possibilities of this overlay.

It is possible to make a highly creative friendship in the overlap of wife and friend. Some very fine creative work can come from this union, generally in the later part of life. Or this overlap may appear simply as companionship between husband and wife, which is one of the finest accomplishments of human relationship.

It would be a fine compliment to a marriage to say that it has culminated in a friendship after the many earlier stages the couple has experienced together. Edward Carpenter observed that one of the highest forms of relationship exists if a husband and wife can tell each other of their affection for another person. This is, indeed, high friendship.

Friendship and Sophia

Sophia and friendship are so nearly alike, though the levels differ, that little but good can come of their overlap. But again, it is good to know what elements are inspiring the exchange and the levels that are involved. Wise are the man and woman who can touch heaven and be conscious enough to give the relationship a form worthy of its power.

CONCLUSION

We have made a modest inquiry into the many levels of femininity that a man experiences in his lifetime. This is always an astonishing survey for a man, since he rarely understands the interior feminine elements that he carries. It taxes most men to the core to differentiate the outer feminine forms that grace his life—mother, wife, sister, daughter, and hetaira—but he is in totally new territory when he discovers the inner forms, which are so close to him he can barely comprehend them. To speak to a man about his inner feminine and describe it as either his guide to the inner world of poetry, his muse or the inspirations that sometimes arise in him, or, in her distorted form, his moods and despair—all of this is a strange and new language for most men.

The hallmark of consciousness in this realm is *differentiation,* and it is this noble faculty that allows a man to see and differentiate his many feminine characteristics. Finely differentiated, the feminine forms attain their highest quality. A golden world of feeling and inspiration opens for a man who is willing to make the effort toward clarity.

This is our modern heroic task. The knights of old donned their helmets and armor, swords and lances, and went out to conquer the world, "out there." The modern hero faces a wealth of possibilities in a new form—the bewildering array of interior feminine elements, which he must rescue, nurture, woo, and protect. This requires a new language and entirely new tools and insights if one is to make his way in the modern world.

Gawain said to King Arthur, "We have won everything by the lance and lost everything by the sword." This is as true for our day as for the chivalric world of our colorful ancestors. The lance is the symbol of differentiation, that fine art of separating and clarifying; the sword is that clumsy male element that would hack its way by brute force through any obstacle. There is far too much sword in our modern character and far too little lance. If a modern man wishes to battle again on heroic soil, it is in the realm of relationship and among the interior elements of femininity where he will find his new role.

As Goethe wrote at the conclusion of his masterpiece, *Faust,* "The Eternal Feminine leads us on."